Hex codes, or hexadecimal codes, are a way to represent colors in digital devices and web design. Each hex code refers to a very specific color. A Hex color is expressed as a six-digit combination of numbers and letters, preceded by a pound sign or hashtag, defined by its mix of red, green, and blue (RGB). The first two letters or numbers refer to red, the next two refer to green, and the last two refer to blue.

The color values are defined as values between 00 and FF. Hex codes are a universal way to describe colors. This book is specifically about neon colors.

A is for amaranth magenta

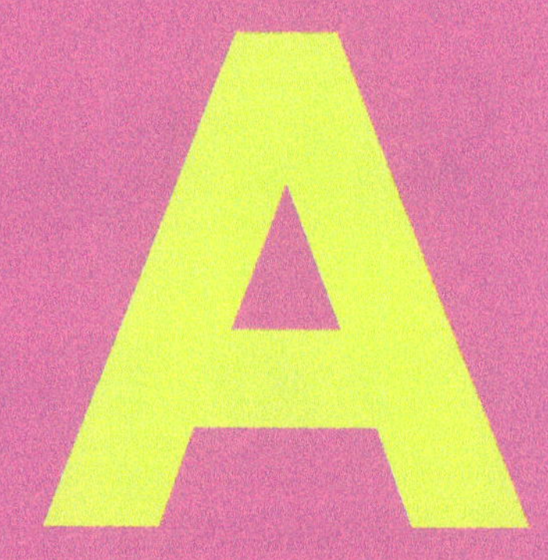

#ED3CCA

a is for arctic lime

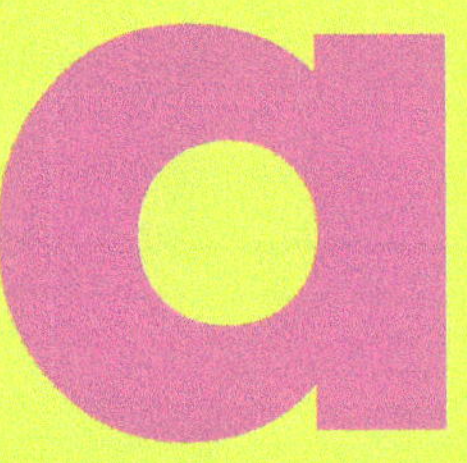

#DOFF14

B is for ball green

B

#22EE33

b is for blaze orange

b

#FF6600

C is for capri

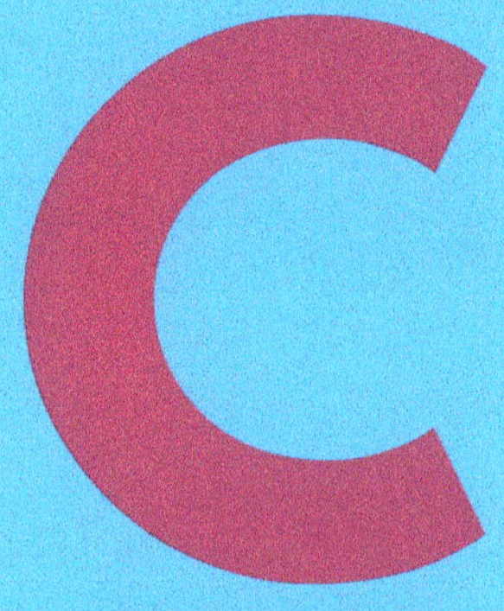

#OOBFFF

c is for cerise

c

#DA3287

D is for daffodil

D

#FFFF31

d is for daisy bush

d

#4F2398

E is for elbas

E

#FFDA03

e is for electric green

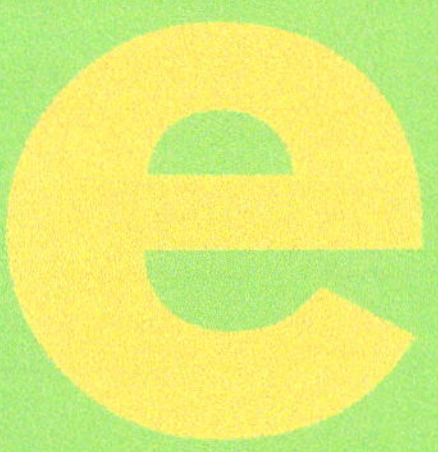

#21FC0D

G is for genie

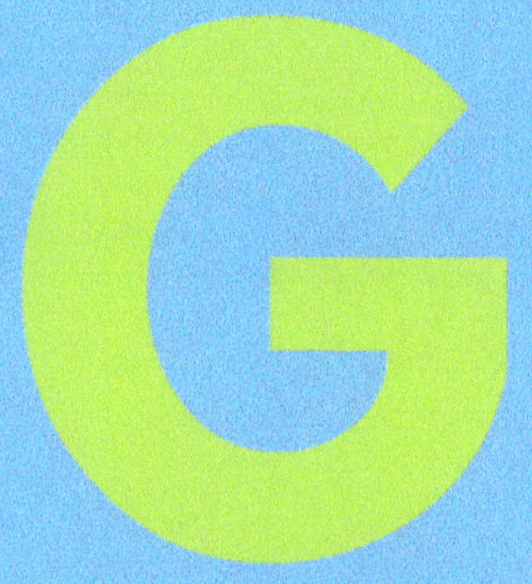

#62B3F2

g is for green lizard

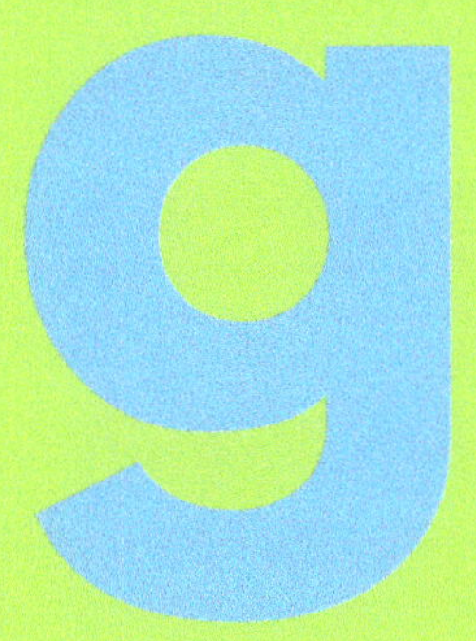

#A7F432

H is for heat wave

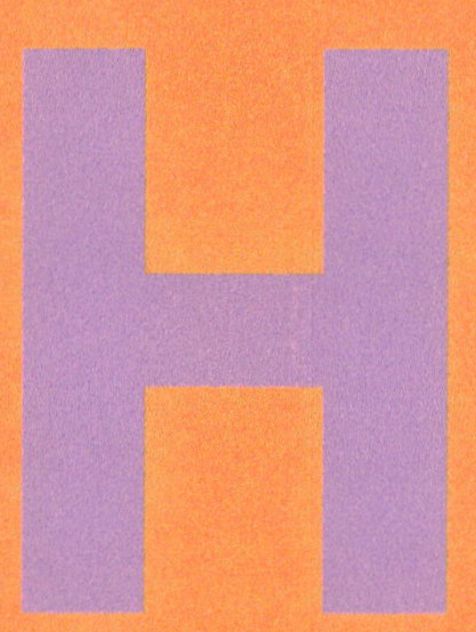

#FF7A00

h is for heliotrope

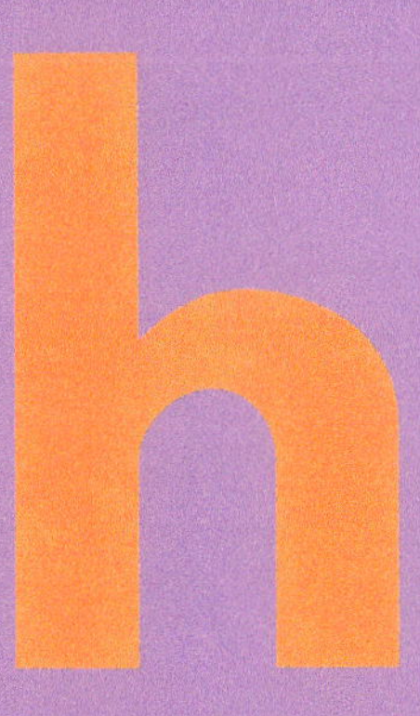

#DF73FF

I is for ibiza lights

I

#FC96FF

i is for indigo

i

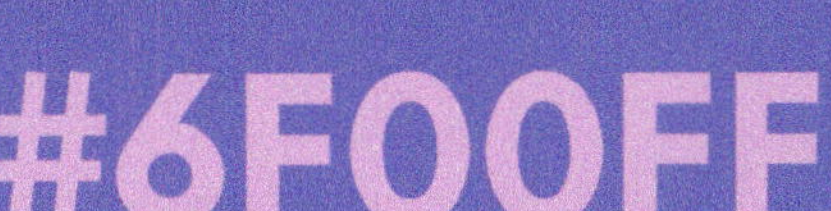

J is for jade glass

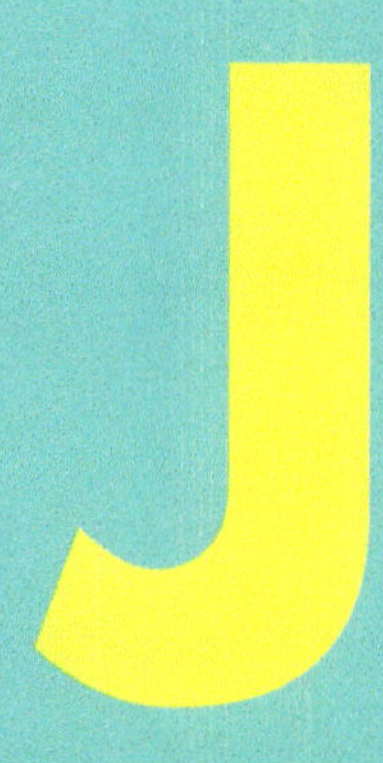

#00CED1

j is for jaune

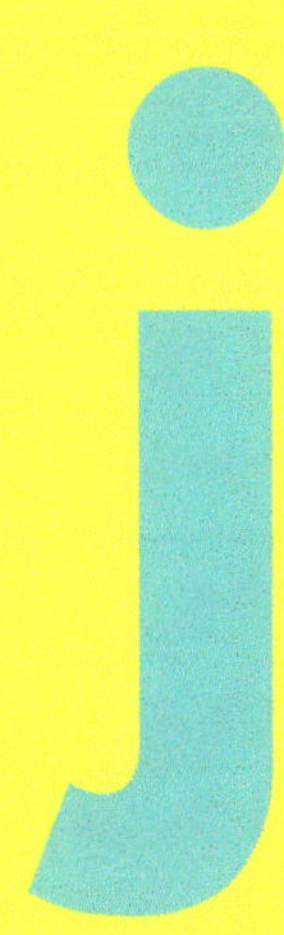

#FFF639

K is for katsure blue

K

#3660AA

k is for kiwi 2

k

#8EE53F

L is for lemon pie

#F1FF62

l is for lime

l

#AAFF32

M is for magenta

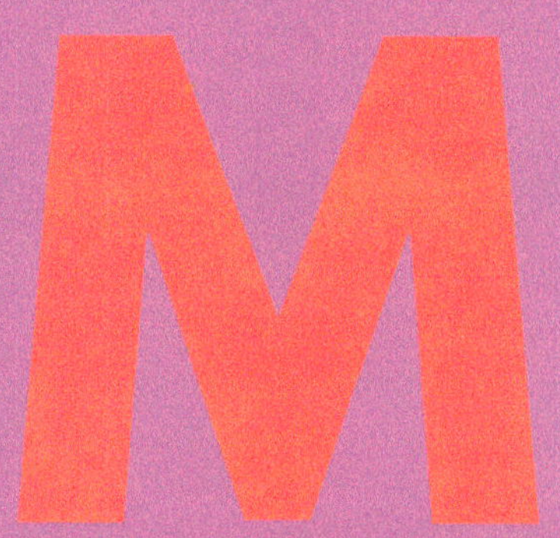

#FF00FF

m is for medium scarlet

m

#FC2847

N is for neon purple

N

#BC13FE

n is for neon yellow

n

#CFFF04

O is for orange glo

#FF6F30

o is for orange juice

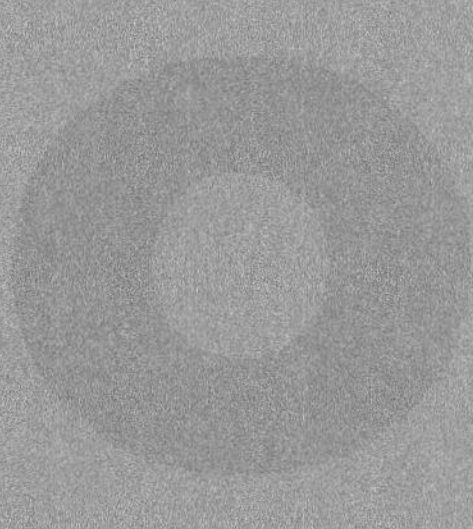

#FF7F00

P is for pink flamingo

P

#FF66FF

p is for pink ink

p

#FF1476

Q is for quartile

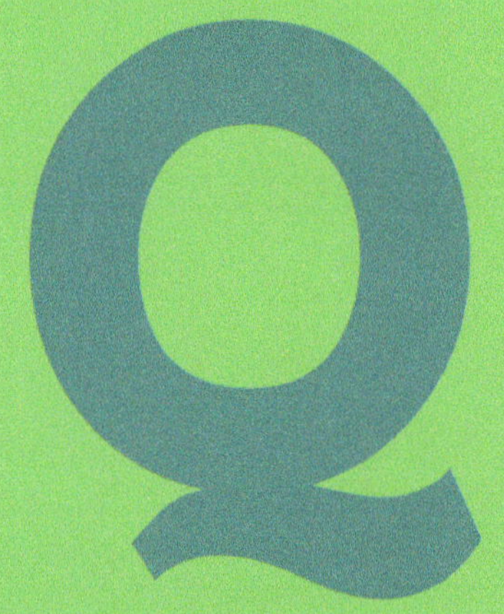

#4CBB17

q is for quetzal teal

q

#007E74

R is for red orange

R

#FF3F34

r is for rio grande

r

#BBD009

S is for shocking pink

S

#FE02A2

s is for spring

s

#00F900

T is for tennis ball

T

#DFFF4F

t is for true blue

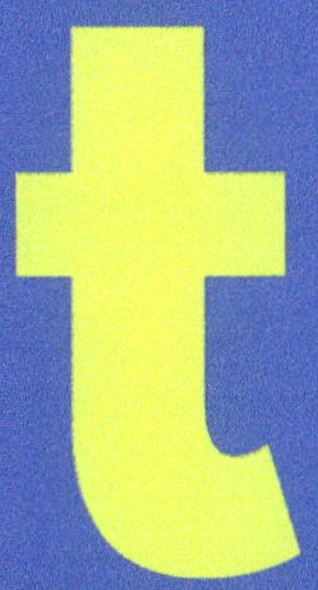

#010FCC

U is for ufo green

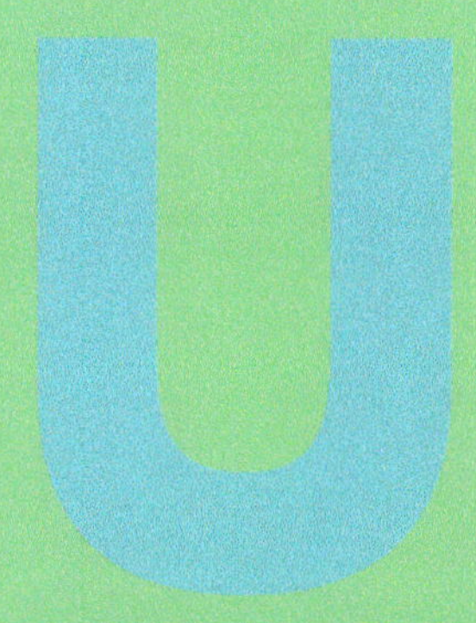

#3CD070

u is for utopia beckons

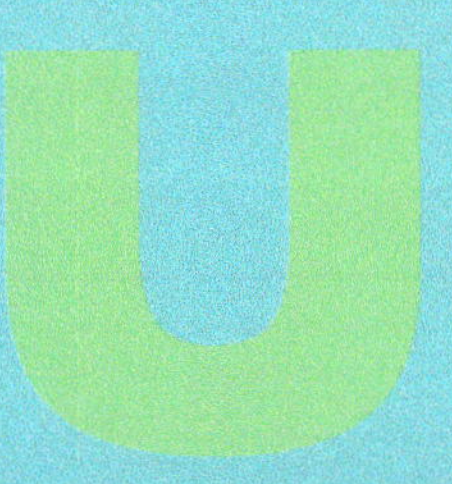

#31B3BE

V is for veronica

V

#A020F0

v is for violet-red

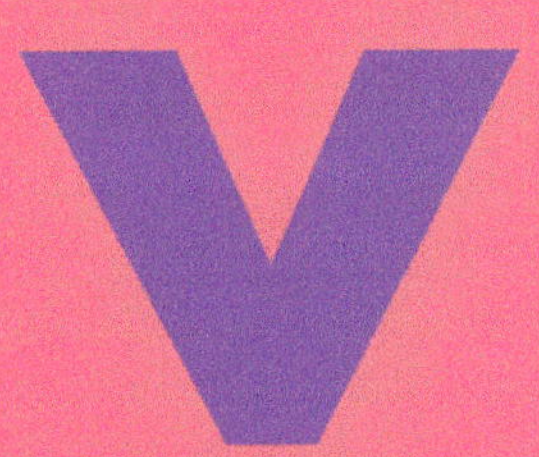

#F75394

W is for wageningen green

W

#34B233

w is for wellywood

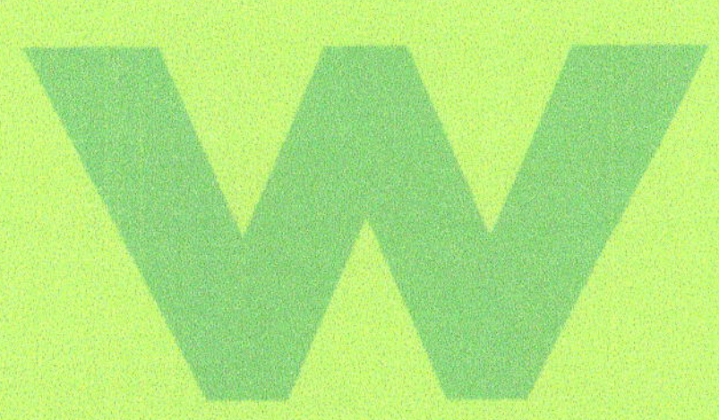

#A3D92D

X is for xanthic

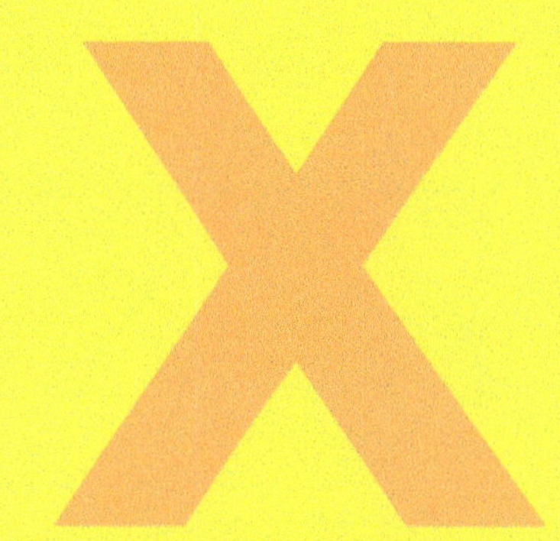

#EEED09

x is for xanthous

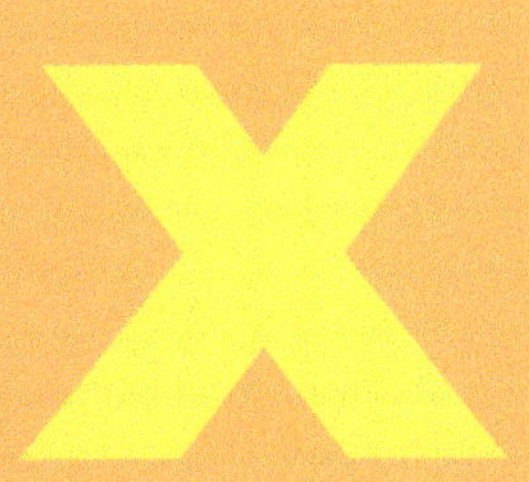

#F5AE2F

Y is for yama light

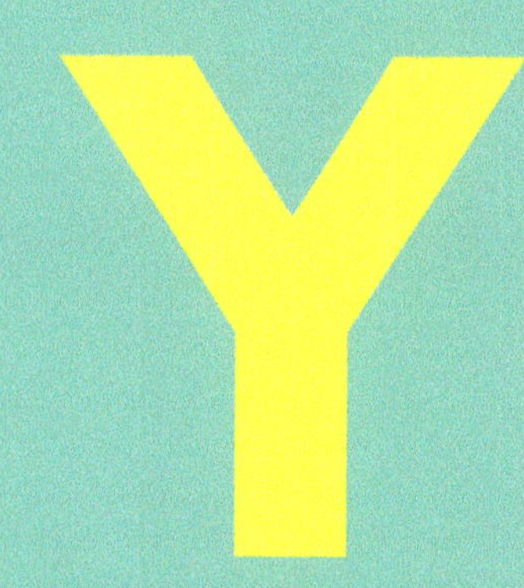

#48BFAB

y is for yellow

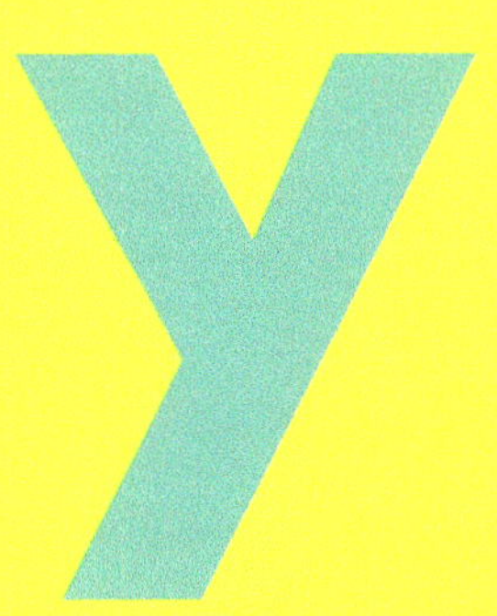

#FFFF00

Z is for zanah

Z

#0014A8

z is for zappo

Z

#FF9215